Pinan Shodan Kata

David Alexander

Caution!

The techniques and theories found within this book are described solely for reference and have been developed and obtained over the years through safe training with professional instructors in a safe environment. The author and publisher accept **no responsibility** whatsoever that may result from practicing/performing the techniques and instructions in this book. Before any change in a fitness regime one would do well in seeking professional advice.

Pain is your body saying "stop", please listen to this warning when training.

PINAN SHODAN KATA

Pinan Shodan Kata "peaceful first degree form"

In many dojos in the west Pinan Shodan Kata is taught as the second kata as it is deemed more difficult than Pinan Nidan kata but it is traditionally the kata for when one obtains their Yellow belt grade.

Pinan Shodan kata encompasses a good arsenal of techniques for the karate practitioner to build on to develop a quick and effective defence against typical attacks such as grabs and swinging punches we could encounter today. Much of this kata emphasises on both arms being utilized simultaneously to maintain a good guard and offensive techniques.

The initial techniques offer one of the most effective guards for close quarter combat with an aggressor and the knife hand blocks offer good defence against hook punches and similar attacks.

Pinan Shodan also encompasses one rather long combination of blocks, strikes and kicks towards the end

1

of the kata. This can be translated/interpreted in many ways but speed and solid techniques is what the main concern is when practising this section. It seems wise that one should separate this section into two (or even more) for realistic applications.

By studying the techniques found within Pinan Shodan it becomes apparent that it encompasses rather simple but effective defensive strikes against a range of attacks, with blocking techniques and stances that can adapt with the attack, no surprise then that it is the first kata one would/should learn.

PINAN SHODAN KATA

1- Facing north, Shoulder width, relaxed stance. Back straight, chin up, and fists clenched and arms slightly bent by the side.

2. Looking west, shift into a left cat stance and simultaneously left arm circular middle body block and right forearm head guard (covering the temple and ear).

3. Continuing west, collapse right forearm down into the left forearm.

4. Continuing west, slide up into shoulder width stance with torso facing north again, and left hammer fist to head level whilst pulling right hand back to the side.

5. Looking east, shift into a right cat stance and simultaneously right arm circular middle body block and left forearm head guard (covering the temple and ear).

6. Continuing east, collapse left forearm down into the right forearm.

7. Continuing east, slide up into shoulder width stance with torso facing north again, and right hammer fist to head level whilst pulling right hand back to the side.

8. Looking south over right shoulder, turn and shift into a right cat stance and simultaneously perform a right middle circular block and right front kick.

9. Turning towards north (after kick), shift into a

left cat stance, and left knife hand block.

10. Advancing north, step forwards into a right cat stance, and right knife hand block.

11. Advancing north, step forwards into a left cat stance, and left knife hand block.

12. Advancing north, step forwards into a right forward leaning stance, and right spear hand to solar plexus height.

13. Looking south-east over left shoulder, shift around and into a left cat stance, and left knife hand block.

14. Advancing south-east, step forwards into a right cat stance, and right knife hand block.

15. Looking south-west over right shoulder, shift into a right cat stance, and right knife hand block.

16. Advancing south-west, step forwards into a left cat stance, and left knife hand block.

17. Looking south over left shoulder, turn towards south into a left forward leaning stance whilst simultaneously sweeping the previous left knife hand block across to the left.

18. Advancing south, right middle circular block, right front kick, on landing throw a left reverse punch.

19. Continuing south, after previous punch, draw back punch and left middle circular block.

20. Advancing south, left front kick, on landing throw a right reverse punch, then step through into a right forward leaning stance and right forearm supported double block.

21. Looking north-west over left shoulder, shift around and into a left forward leaning stance facing north-west, left lower block, step forwards into a right stance, right head block.

22. Looking north-east over right shoulder, shift around and into a right forward leaning stance facing north-east, right lower block, step forwards into a left stance, left head block.

End of Pinan Shodan kata

4

Pinan Shodan Kata:

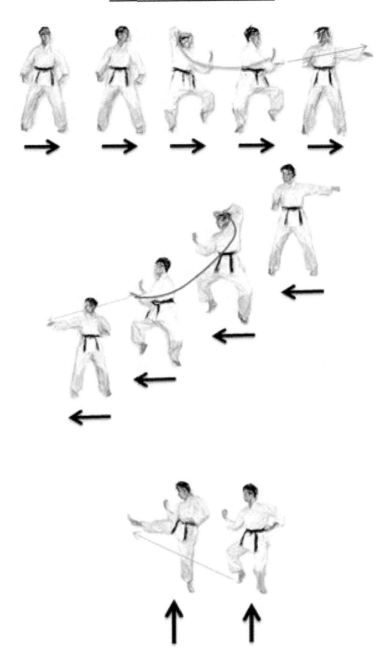

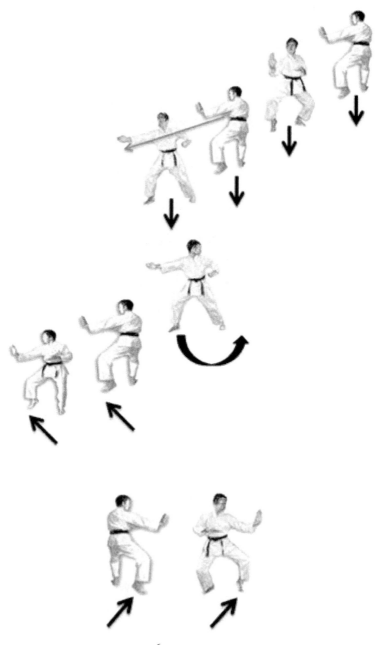

Pinan Shodan Kata

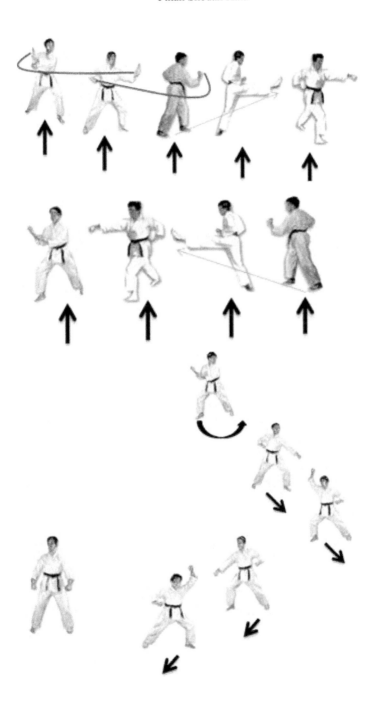

PINAN SHODAN KATA ANALYSIS

Stances:
1.   Cat stance.
2.   Forward leaning stance.
3.   Shoulder width stance.

Blocks:
1.   Dual blocking/guard, middle circular block and right forearm head guard.
2.   Middle circular block
3.   Knife hand block/strike
4.   Supported forearm block
5.   Lower block
6.   Head block

Strikes/Kicks:
1.   Inner forearm strike (1st combination) could also be interpreted as a stomach corkscrew punch.
2.   Hammer fist
3.   Front kick
4.   Spear hand
5.   Reverse punch

Pinan Shodan effectively teaches one to defend against the following violent attacks. Of course, this again is subject to one's personal interpretation but it is probably fair to suggest that the following attacks can be realistically defended from utilizing the techniques found within Pinan Shodan.

- Common hook punch volleys
- Stepping punches
- Kicks
- Neck grabs
- Lapel grabs
- Wrist grabs
- Attacks from behind

BUNKAI FROM PINAN SHODAN KATA

Techniques 1-7:
· **An aggressor has thrown a common hook punch towards you (let us assume a right hand punch):** Assume the cat stance to avoid the punch and simultaneously guiding the punch around in front of you (from your left to right) with your right arm and grab the opponents wrist (utilizing all this in one motion will hopefully cause your opponent to lose their balance). Then slam your left outer forearm into the opponents elbow. This alone can break the elbow or secure an arm lock on the opponent as they collapse under their own momentum. Follow through this defence by raising your stance as the kata suggests into a shoulder width stance and slam your left hammer fist towards your opponents face (be sure to maintain the initial wrist grab you have secured). If you follow through with the hammer fist and are secure in the shoulder width stance this will cause the opponent the fall backwards, thus completing your defence.

Techniques 1-7:

An aggressor has thrown a common hook punch towards you (let us assume a right hand punch) with the intentions of throwing his left: Advance forwards into a cat stance raising your guard as suggested in techniques 2+5 to defend against the attack and any possible follow through attacks. This will bring you inside of your opponent's punch. Now bring your current right hand/forearm head guard down into a fist strike up and into your opponent's solar plexus (aiming to "wind" them). Then depending on what "feels" most efficient at this point perhaps complete the combination either by an elbow strike towards your opponents head or complete as the kata suggests in this section with a hammer fist to the head/neck (techniques 4+7). Basically this style of defence found within Pinan Shodan kata allows you to "get in close" inside of your opponents reach, but you must be sure to throw effective close quarter strikes until the opponent yields or collapses, and the initial double hand block and guard in techniques 2+5 position your arms to both protect your vital areas and allows you to counter with hammer fists, back fists, elbow strikes and short punches.

Technique 8:

This section of Pinan Shodan kata could be interpreted simply as a block of a punch (high or low) and countering with a groin kick from the leading posed leg in the cat stance form.

Techniques 9-16:

This section of Pinan Shodan especially emphasizes the utilization of open handed knife strikes and blocks. Where the applications can vary from grab escapes, punch blocking and striking. By studying the following interpretations one can gain and understanding of further applications from the knife hand blocks/strikes and spear

11

hand techniques. In the katas to come after Pinan Shodan where similar combinations of knife hand blocks may be found, one can interpret them the same way or following the trend/style of the practised kata where they are found. Because we find this style of defence using a cat stance and knife hand blocks/strikes in other katas we can be sure that these techniques were considered an essential and flexible self-defence against an attack. Studying other kata with this technique within it can increase ones understanding, which will develop more applications following other kata trends and styles of defence and attack.

An aggressor has thrown a common hook punch towards you (let us assume a right hand punch) with the intentions of following through with more attacks. You have two options:
1. Defend inside of the attack
2. Or outside of the attack

Defending yourself inside of the attack by utilizing the knife hand block in the style of this section of the kata is tactically less efficient. Aim to first avoid the attack by shifting off the centre of their attack and block the punch at their wrist/forearm with a left knife hand block (essentially you want to be striking their own attack) and simultaneously grab the blocked arm, and remember to utilize a pulling motion developed from the transition into a cat stance. Then bring your right hand across and over their arm you have secured momentarily and strike their neck with the second knife hand strike…upon impact, be sure to pull on the left grabbed arm you have in a bow like action to twist your opponent, thus exposing the neck further and preventing them from countering with their free hand. One could also include the spear hand strike from Pinan Shodan kata at this point to complete the defence, by releasing the grabbed arm after the neck strike and follow through with the already chambered left hand into a spear hand strike again to the opponent's neck, simultaneously pulling down on the opponent's head after the previous right knife hand strike to this area again exposes the neck further. One could also perform a throwing technique by looping the opponent's head after the right knife hand strike to the neck *see Pinan Sandan interpretation of technique 1-7.*

Defending yourself outside of the punch with the knife hand blocking combination found in this section of Pinan Shodan is far more efficient, and one can utilize the similar defence as option one here, but being on the outside of the attack naturally allows you to gain an advantage with less effort as it is far more difficult for the opponent to follow through with his free hand. But gaining this advantageous position can be difficult against circular punch therefore there are two methods:

1. Shifting into cat stance to avoid the punch by guiding the arc of the attack in front of you and simultaneously blocking with a right knife hand (*in the correct form, as in first bringing the hand towards your ear to snap it back out towards your target. This motion naturally defends you from the punch in the avoidance movement of your defence.*) to block the punch by their wrist and simultaneously transform the striking style block into a grab.

2. Shift into a left cat stance and block and grab the attack with a left knife hand and, then transfer the grab to the right hand (*in the correct form of a knife hand block, as in first bringing the hand towards your ear to snap it back out towards your target*) and sweep the arm around to the right and shift/step into a right cat stance whilst maintaining this grip of their wrist.

Whichever technique you utilize to obtain this position outside of the opponents defence continue by pulling the grabbed arm towards you and utilize your left hand as the second knife hand block as a strike to the opponent's

13

elbow to potentially break it whilst you compensate for their resistance to this strike with your current grab of their wrist. This will no doubt collapse your opponent if done correctly towards the direction of their momentum. At this point you may simply follow through with this left knife hand strike to the elbow to secure an arm lock, or again utilize the right hand as a spear hand technique, this time either simply at their neck or past it at the inside of their throat area   then pull on their neck to take them down in a fashion that is awkward to them in the opposite direction of your previous arm-lock (*as the human body cannot cope very well with two forces as it makes the opponents balance easier to manipulate*).

Techniques 17-18:
An aggressor has thrown a common hook punch towards you (let us assume a right hand punch) with the intentions of throwing his left: Sweep your left knife hand block/guide as suggested as section number 17 suggests to first block the opponent's attack. Then bring your right circular block under the opponent's punch and bring around to your right in front of you and then transform the circular block into a grab. Then utilize the front kick then land the kick and complete this section with the reverse punch to the side of the opponent's head or the side of the body (kidneys). The kick in this section may realistically be interpreted as a side kick whilst you would hike back on the opponent's arm for balance as you continue your grip.

Techniques 19-20
An aggressor has thrown a common hook punch towards you (let us assume a right hand punch) with the intentions of throwing his left: Avoid the punch to the outside and simultaneously apply a middle circular block and grab the punch. Then utilize the front kick then land the kick and complete this section with the reverse

punch to the side of the opponent's head or the side of the body (kidneys). Again, the kick in this section may realistically be interpreted as a side kick whilst you would hike back on the opponent's arm as you continue your grip. Then whilst maintaining the grip of your opponents arm with your original right hand block (and while you should still find yourself on the outside of your opponent's attack). Bring your left hand to the captured arm then take your opponent backwards as a takedown, be sure to secure this arm lock throughout the entire takedown.

Techniques 21-22

This section of Pinan Shodan can be applied to a defence against a kick or a punch:

An aggressor has thrown a common hook punch towards you (let us assume a right hand punch) with the intentions of throwing his left: Utilizing the full motion of the lower block, bring your right arm around the outside of the punch to first intercept and circle away from you to your right then grip the wrist and twist the opponents arm whilst simultaneously bringing your left free hand into a lower block onto their elbow to lock/break the arm collapsing the opponent. Then complete the combination with the head block as a strike using your right forearm as a strike to the back of the neck.

An aggressor has launched a kick towards you (let us assume a right leg kick): Avoid the kick and aim to deflect the kick with a left lower block. Then instantly stride forward into a right head block utilizing this technique as a strike to the opponents neck. It is possible at this point to follow through with similar blocks as strikes to the groin or neck/head with further lower blocks and head blocks and close quarter strikes as suggested in Pinan Shodan kata.

BUNKAI FROM LOCKS AND GRABS

Techniques 1-7 from Pinan Shodan kata:
An aggressor has grabbed your neck or lapel with
one hand (let us assume their left hand as most would
prefer to punch with their right fist, as it would seem
most people are right handed) and is about to punch
you with their free hand they have posed ready. You
may even be pushed against a wall (common street
attack 6+7 listed in chapter 31 *common street attacks we are*
faced with today):   As soon as you can possibly
retaliate, instantly drop down and back into a cat stance
and simultaneously bring your guard up as suggested in
techniques 2+5 of Pinan Shodan, one arm either side of
your opponent's hold on you (this will protect your face
from their punch if/when thrown) and slam your right
inner forearm as hard as you can against the opponent's
outstretched arm aiming for his wrist as you secure the
inside of their elbow joint from compensating (gathering
power into this strike from the shift of weight into your cat
stance).   This motion should collapse their arm at the
elbow, freeing the hold.   This motion of defence will
naturally chamber your right forearm for a hammer fist
strike to their head which should be employed instantly

once you are free. The entire style of this combination helps prevent the opponent launching his punch.

Technique 8 from Pinan Shodan kata:
An aggressor from behind you has taken hold of your right shoulder attempting to pull you around to face them: Simultaneously drop your weight and shift around clockwise and utilize the circular block found in this section of Pinan Shodan to break their hold, then launch a kick to their groin from the leading posed leg in the cat stance form.

Techniques 1-7 from Pinan Shodan kata:
An aggressor has taken hold of your wrist, either with one or both of their hands:
You are now perhaps contemplating that this section of Pinan Shodan kata appears to have endless applications. This escape technique from an arm/wrist grab relies on the power and twist from the forearm inner strike together with the shift into cat stance. Essentially if it is your left arm that is grabbed, simultaneously shift back into a cat stance and slam your right inner forearm into the wrist/s of your opponent and "roll" over their grip and once your free instantly bring the right arm back to your left side to chamber a hammer fist to the opponent' neck (this motion of chambering the strike will draw you closer to your opponent and defend yourself from a potential punch).

Techniques in section 8 from Pinan Shodan kata:
An aggressor has taken hold of your wrist, either with one or both of their hands:
Due to the cat stance in this section of Pinan Shodan, one could apply this section in a defence against an aggressor's hold of the wrist/forearm, where the shift of weight into a cat stance with a swift middle body block motion to break or loosen the opponent's grip, then utilize a front kick to the groin area (groin kick variation where

17

the roof of the foot is used instead of the ball of the foot). Although this method of escape requires the karateka to utilize an amount of strength for this to work, the groin kick is what is emphasised here in one's defence.

Techniques 9-16 from Pinan Shodan kata:

An aggressor has taken hold of your wrist, either with one or both of their hands: This section of Pinan Shodan kata (and indeed where you would find the knife hand block/strike in other katas) the emphasis is on knife hand blocks and the power from a cat stance. A defence from such an attack can be performed utilizing this section of Pinan Shodan. Utilize a swift transition into a cat stance down and back, simultaneously circle your trapped arm's wrist in a motion which will encompass your weight shift to free your hand (*please understand that this technique is extremely difficult to explain using pen and paper, but if you practice on a none compliant partner with an instructor this circular motion of the wrist and draw back with a knife hand will free you from any persons grip*), this will either free your hand or you will partially free your hand and end up with a grab of your opponents wrist instead, then instantly snap your other hand as a knife hand strike towards the opponent's neck (or spear hand to the neck). One may even utilize your free hand as a knife hand block as a strike to the opponent's elbow to potentially break it whilst you compensate for their resistance to this strike with your current grab of their wrist.

Notes

_____

_____

_____

_____

_____

_____

_____

_____

_____

_____

_____

_____

_____

_____

_____

David Alexander

ABOUT THE AUTHOR

David Alexander has trained in karate most of his life. He
has published numerous resources on the subject.

Other books available on Amazon:

Karate in Modern day use

Shukokai Karate Kata

This booklet is part of the Shukokai kata booklet series

Printed in Great Britain
by Amazon